I Will Tell You Of
PEACH STONE

I Will Tell You Of

Lothrop, Lee & Shepard Co. • A Division of William Morrow & Co., Inc. • New York

PEACH STONE

by Nathan Zimelman · illustrated by Haru Wells

1 2 3 4 5 80 79 78 77 76
Library of Congress Cataloging in Publication Data
Zimelman, Nathan. I will tell you of Peach Stone.
SUMMARY: An old man and his dog gain immortality by bringing the gift of the
peach from China to the rest of the world.
[1. Peach—Fiction] I. Wells, Haru, illus. II. Title.
PZ7.Z57Iac   [E]   74-7192
ISBN 0-688-41662-4   ISBN 0-688-51662-9 (lib. bdg.)

To George Mack, who likes books

Once upon a time when the moon was young there lived in China a man so old that no one knew what his name had been, and even he had long ago forgotten it.

When of a summer morning he walked down the village street, the merchants called out from their doorways, "Welcome, welcome, Old Man. Come and sip a cup of tea."

Happy was the man in whose shop Old Man stopped. Among the merchants it was said that he who was visited by Old Man in the morning would have a golden afternoon.

In the afternoon when school was over, Old Man could be found in the village square surrounded by the children. Even little Wang Lo whose head always turned away from his teacher, Mr. Yen, whenever a bird flew past an open school window, sat unmoving while Old Man told his wonderful tales. Old Man spoke of the creation of the sun, of how man came upon the earth, and of the many wondrous things that he and he alone knew.

When evening touched Old Man's slippers with its shadowy fingers and the children were called to their homes, he sighed, groaned, and rose to his feet. Then, followed by his dog, he slowly left the village.

While the moon looked down upon his little house, he prepared a dinner of rice and tea and talked of the day to his dog Peach Stone.

Peach Stone had been so named because, in all of China, he alone loved to eat the great golden peach down to its crinkled stone. When Old Man talked, Peach Stone would listen and understand in a dog's way.

Old Man wished to go on forever in the pleasant mornings with the merchants and the joyful afternoons with the children. As he did each year, he forgot that soon there must be rains and chill winds.

One morning when he awoke to the hope of another day, the rain had driven the sun from the sky. Through every chink in Old Man's house the wind whistled, "Here, here, I am here."

"Soon," Old Man said to himself, "soon the rain and wind will go away and I will again walk down the village street. The merchants will call out. And when the noon has passed, the children will run from the schoolhouse and sit at Old Man's feet and hear my stories."

The wind blew, "No-o-o-o, no-o-o-o-o." And the rain splashed its droplets through the thatch roof.

Even on the days when no rain fell on the earth and the wind had blown itself breathless, the weak sun could not draw the merchants away from their charcoal stoves to stand in cold doorways and call out their greetings to Old Man.

Even little Wang Lo knew that when the sun is only a tiny lemon drop, the cold turns small noses red. Then it is best to stay warm before a merry fire.

When Old Man came to the village square, there was not one shivering child waiting to be warmed by his wondrous stories. Perhaps because he did not wish to remember, Old Man had forgotten the way of people in the winter.

Long before the early evening shadows told Old Man it was time to go home, he and Peach Stone left the village. Followed by their breaths which hung in white puffs above their heads, they walked slowly back to Old Man's house.

Each day Old Man prepared his bowl of rice and cup of tea. But now he often forgot to eat. "Peach Stone," he would sigh, "who will remember Old Man when he is gone if the village forgets Old Man when he is here? Only Peach Stone will remember Old Man, and you too are old. Soon Old Man will be forgotten as if he had never been."

Peach Stone, who understood as only a dog can, came to Old Man and laid his head on Old Man's knee. And for a moment Old Man forgot that he was lonely.

But soon the snow covered the path. Now Old Man could not go to the village. His sighs grew deeper and deeper until one day he could not remember the taste of joy. It was then that he noticed Peach Stone.

Old Man had seen Peach Stone every Monday through Sunday of every year of Peach Stone's life, but this time it was different. Peach Stone had just eaten the very last of the long summer's carefully hoarded golden peaches down to its crinkled stone.

There was little joy in the day but Peach Stone's happiness, while he ate the last peach, brought with it a smile that tickled Old Man's lips and made him laugh. "Peach Stone, Peach Stone, what if this were a land where the peach did not grow? How sad that would be!"

Peach Stone ignored the question and pushed the stone with his nose. It was his way of asking for another golden peach. But there were to be no more peaches for Peach Stone that evening or any other evening until the summer.

"A land where the peach does not grow," Old Man repeated to himself. "The Great Book of Wisdom says that only in China does the peach grow."

Then Old Man had such an idea that he could see nothing else for the wonder of it.

"To work! To work!" cried Old Man.

Peach Stone barked two times, which was his way of saying, "Yes."

The months passed while Old Man and Peach Stone made their preparations. Then at last, the calendar that hung on the wall of Li Po, the grocer, said that spring had come.

One morning a golden sun rose over the village and touched the merchants with warm thoughts of golden coins ringing on their counters. The children were closed within the four walls of the school, but spring tapped at the window and called, "Look, look!"

Mr. Yen, the schoolmaster, had been a boy himself and had never forgotten the excitement of spring. When his small students found a hundred excuses to pass the open window, he understood.

Of course it was little Wang Lo who first saw Old Man and cried, "Look, oh look outside the window! Never, never have you seen what I see now!"

The children pushed and pulled at each other to find a place to see. It was truly a sight to wonder at.

Old Man was walking down the village street, as he had many times before. But this time was not as before. Old Man had always worn a blue cotton robe faded almost to white. Now he wore a silken robe the color of a peach when it is ripe with juice.

Always before, Old Man had walked down the

road with Peach Stone sniffing busily behind him. This time Old Man pulled a gaily painted cart. On the cart was a boat just large enough for one man and one dog. In the boat sat Peach Stone, freshly washed and combed and looking neither to right nor left. And between his paws was one large golden peach stone.

Round about Peach Stone were arranged a cask of the clearest well water and wicker baskets filled with rice, nuts, tea, ginger, and other supplies for a long journey.

Out the door ran the children calling, "What are you doing, Old Man? What are you doing?"

By now they had come to the banks of the Little Yangtze River, which flowed through the village.

Old Man stopped.

Everyone stopped with him and waited to see what he would do.

Old Man lifted the skirts of his beautiful robe. Holding the silken cloth in one hand, he grasped the rope of the cart in the other and pulled it into the Little Yangtze until the water touched the tiny boat.

Softly he lifted the boat and its precious cargo free of the cart.

The river held the boat still until Old Man had carefully boarded. Then the river began to carry the boat away on its long journey.

"Goodbye. Goodbye," Old Man called to the villagers. "The Little Yangtze carries us to the Great Yangtze. Together they will bring us to the ocean on which our ship will sail until we come to a land where the peach does not grow. There we will plant the peach stone.

"The Great Book of Wisdom says that the bringer of gifts will make a safe journey. When in far distant years a child holds the roundness of summer's first

peach, that child will be glad and remember the bringers of the gift, and Peach Stone and Old Man will never be forgotten."

Peach Stone barked goodbye. Slowly the boat moved away from the villagers until, as if it heard the call of the Great Yangtze, the Little Yangtze began to hurry the boat along. While everyone watched, it sailed away.

Although Mr. Yen, who was also a reader of the Great Book of Wisdom, was certain that Old Man and Peach Stone were off to good adventure and warm welcome, he found a tear forming in each of his eyes. He realized how much he and the village would miss Old Man and Peach Stone.

"Mr. Yen, Mr. Yen," Wang Lo called, "the sun has passed the time of school."

"What more could be told this day?" asked Mr. Yen.

"A story," cried little Wang Lo.

"A story! A story!" cried the children.

"Old Man is gone. Who is there left wise enough to tell stories?"

"The teacher," said little Wang Lo.

Mr. Yen smiled away his tears.

"I will tell you the story of Peach Stone and Old Man, how they sailed to strange lands and of their many wonderful adventures," he said.

"Will all the stories be true?" asked Wang Lo.

"As with all stories, in time they will be true."

And since Mr. Yen was a teacher and very wise, they were.

About the Author and Artist

Nathan Zimelman, a native of Sacramento, California, is a graduate of the University of California at Berkeley. The author of twelve other books for children, Mr. Zimelman lives in Sacramento where he devotes full time to his writing.

Haru Wells was born in Buenos Aires, Argentina. After studying and teaching art in Buenos Aires and London, England, she came to New York City, where she has lived ever since. In addition to her work in the design and illustration of children's books, Ms. Wells has created material for television commercials, film and Sesame Street.

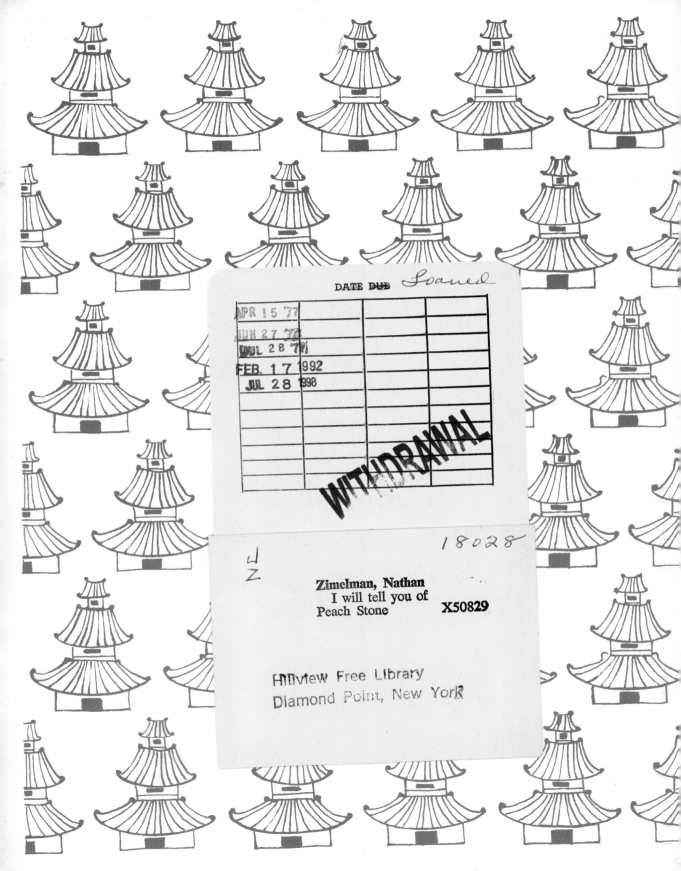